OVERCOME YOUR *Thirst*

A JOURNEY TO FINDING LIFE'S FULFILLMENT

PHOENICIA E. WARNER

WESTBOW
PRESS®
A DIVISION OF THOMAS NELSON
& ZONDERVAN

WestBow Press books may be ordered through booksellers or by contacting:

WestBow Press
A Division of Thomas Nelson & Zondervan
1663 Liberty Drive
Bloomington, IN 47403
www.westbowpress.com
1 (866) 928-1240

ISBN: 978-1-5127-3110-1 (sc)
ISBN: 978-1-5127-3111-8 (e)

Library of Congress Control Number: 2016902456

Print information available on the last page.

WestBow Press rev. date: 06/01/2016

This book is dedicated to the late

Cheryl Felicia King

who went home to be with the Lord before its completion.

Although you are no longer here, I could still hear the wonderful words of encouragement that you consistently gave.

It is also dedicated to my princess *She'Naajah Warner* who has always been my shining star even when the days grew dim. I love you dearly.

Finally, it is dedicated to all those who have committed to joining this journey to finding life's fulfillment. As you read, may you find the satisfaction that you have been seeking out of life.

Enjoy! Be Blessed, and most of all, Be Transformed!

CONTENTS

Acknowledgements xi

Preface xiii

Introduction xv

Chapter 1   Are you thirsty? 1

Chapter 2   Private Practice 11

Chapter 3   Extraordinary Encounters 16

Chapter 4   Life and Light - Oasis or Mirage 22

Chapter 5   H-2-O (Hydration - to - Overflow) 32

Chapter 6   Wells vs. Springs 37

Chapter 7   Drink 47

Chapter 8   Let It Go! 54

Epilogue: A New Thirst 61

ACKNOWLEDGEMENTS

At the completion of this project and assignment, I stand in acknowledgement of Jehovah God and His Holy Spirit for providing all that I needed to fulfill this task in one way or another.

First for the revelation of His Word, and the ability to get it from heart-form, to book-form, I am grateful. I acknowledge and give thanks for His guidance that was provided every step of the way, and for the many persons that He has sent along the way to give assistance, support and encouragement.

I acknowledge my husband for being the motivational force that caused me to remain true to the woman that God has created me to be, and for the constant reminder to stay focused on the purpose that God has placed on my life. To my sister Val who contributed her editorial services, Cassi who kept me on task, my Mother, Eileen Warner and everyone who believed in me and offered other assistance in any way, my heart is overwhelmed with gratitude. Special thanks to Robert Oxendine for the Author's Photo. There is not enough time or pages that would allow me to make mention of every name, but if you know who you are, please note that I could not have done this without you, and would like for you to accept my humble word of thanks!

PREFACE

It was a day like any other day on my thirty-minute break from the demands that came from life as a care-giver at the child-care facility where I had been employed for less than two months at that time. Although the much needed break was only but a half hour long, I often used the time to regroup and reenergize. The peace that came with sitting in silence, usually in my car or at a nearby park, was incredible. Many days I would take advantage of the aura of tranquillity, by getting into the Word of God and simply communing with my Heavenly Father.

During this particular break, I chose to do some reading, and in consideration of the amount of time that I had to play with, it was one of those moments where I decided to read from a page that I randomly flipped the old tattered Bible open to. After one flip, a very familiar scripture jumped off of the page and immediately got my attention. It was the story of the Woman at the Well. As much as I had read and heard many references made to this particular scripture, the download of revelation that I received once I read the words that seemed to be floating off the pages, was both new and fresh to me. It was as if I had read the story for the first time in my life. Not only did it become fresh, I immediately realized how much the life of the Woman at the Well was still present and overwhelmingly represented in our lives today. Very specifically, that very evening, I had been invited to a conference call where the participants had been sharing about their lives and how un-fulfilled they had been. It was as if I was given the antidote to their seemingly un-going misery during my thirty-minute break that day.

Since then, I had encountered so many situations I could apply the revelation that I had received to, that one day, I decided to write it down. It seemed as if everything that I heard around me pointed to what I had received that day. As years passed, the demand to share what I had written became stronger, and after seeking the Lord for the answer to the question "Why?", I was instructed to turn the fifteen pages of information that I had written down, into a full-fledged book.

Although this was not really the beginning, it was a pivotal point in this venture because, once I agreed to take on the assignment to develop what was revealed to me that day, into a book, it was then that I was taken deeper into revelation in ways that were unimaginable. The parallel between specific ideas, events and conversations was made clearer as I read, prayed and ultimately began putting pen to paper. I realized more and more what the well-read story really meant, and how it was still very relevant today.

Overcome your Thirst, is a journey that can be taken that would unveil the underlying yearnings in your life, unmask the exhaustion of temporary fulfillment and ultimately point to the only source of eternal satisfaction, which was only revealed during the final stages of writing the book. It is also a journey that allows you the opportunity to ponder questions that were designed to help you capture where you really are, while propelling you closer to your point of discovering the one thing that would give you true fulfillment. There are also spaces provided for the purpose of journaling your thoughts while growing and developing as you read and reflect. Along the journey, you will also encounter examples of situations that will give you the comfort in knowing that you are really not alone in your wilderness or the only one experiencing dry and empty patches in life.

It is my earnest prayer that by the end of the book, you would have discovered the areas of your life where your thirst lies. I also pray that you would have been propelled to take the necessary steps that would allow you to truly walk into the blessed and fulfilled life that you were destined to have. Read and be blessed!

INTRODUCTION

Have you ever had one of your daily activities interrupted by great thirst? Were you ever so thirsty that everything had to be put on hold until you got yourself something to drink? What about the kind of thirst that caused your tongue to be stuck to the roof of your mouth and the walls of your throat seemed to be sticking together because there were no signs of moisture? No matter the degree, we have all experienced thirst at some point in time, and we can all attest to the fact that it is indeed very uncomfortable, and more so, it has attached to it, the great need to be satisfied.

Thirst is defined by the Webster's Dictionary as "An uncomfortable dry feeling in the throat and mouth, accompanied by an urgent desire for liquids." Thirst acts as an indicator which alerts us of a deficiency of liquid in our body. It yearns for satisfaction, and is usually followed by an act that would seek to bring just that. At times, just having any drink would simply ease the yearning, but there are times you are so thirsty, the only thing that would give you any kind of satisfaction is a drink of pure refreshing water.

Just as our bodies thirst, as humans we experience great yearnings in our inner beings, that we spend our time, energy and in many cases, lots of money, trying to satisfy. These yearnings may present themselves through a variety of ways within the many facets that join and work together to make up who we are as individuals. We can identify them by a feeling of emptiness, a void or a great need that we might experience, and in almost every instance, once that longing is felt, we set out to fill it. Although every person is different and each circumstance is very unique, as humans we experience varying degrees of emptiness that we long to be filled in one way or another. If you have ever experienced this feeling of needing that one thing, person or activity that you are convinced will provide the satisfaction that you need, then you definitely know what it means to be thirsty.

The Woman at the Well in scripture also had a great need. She experienced great thirst and found herself along with her water-pot, at a well where she had intentions of drawing water. She felt that having a drink of that water was necessary to quench the thirst that she felt within. It was at this same well on one of her many visits, that she encountered the kind of fulfillment that would satisfy her once and for all. She came face to face with what she really needed, and did what was necessary to bring about the kinds of changes in her life that she desired for so long.

As we are in every instance, she was faced with varying options of quenchers. Perhaps it was similar to a choice between having a soda-pop and getting a drink of pure refreshing water. Instead of doing what she always did by reaching for what could only bring her temporary satisfaction, she made a conscious decision to activate and utilize the very thing that would bring her the kind of satisfaction that she had been searching for all along – Everlasting Satisfaction!

~ CHAPTER 1 ~

Are you thirsty?

T he Woman at the Well in the story that was recorded in the fourth chapter of the Gospel of John, had experienced some of the same thirst that we experience in our lives. As a matter of fact, the story took place at the well where she had gone to draw water. It is easy to assume that she was in fact *thirsty* because of her actions. She had actually put one foot in front of the other to do the thing that she thought necessary in order to quench her thirst. We do not know how far she lived from the well that she went to draw water from, but we do know that she actually left the shelter of her home to get what she thought was necessary to fill her need. She performed an action which was indicative of the fact that she was in need of this water. It is also safe to assume that it was by no means her first trip to this particular well, especially since she displayed her rights and privilege to the well when she declared that it was given to her people by their fore-father Jacob (John 4:12). So although she left her house to go there, she felt right at home and comfortable enough to take a drink.

Sometimes, it is very easy to identify whether or not we are thirsty or the degree to which we are yearning, by the things that we do. Our actions can definitely point to the fact that we are indeed thirsty. However, it is not always that easy to identify. After doing the same things repeatedly for some time, the actions in some way become the norm or what can be perceived as the way of life for many of us. Sometimes these actions have become so comfortable that we tend to

1

feel right at home when we carry them out. They have become so much a part of life that we do not know whether or not we do them in order to quench a thirst within, which in some cases can be very subtle and underlying, as in the following examples.

~~~~~~~~~

You may know someone who have found themselves between a rock and a hard place, where on one end they are loyal and dedicated to one relationship after the next, although they continue to be placed in a position of self-denial and compromise. The relationship that they end up entertaining, demands that they go against certain standards that they have covertly set for their lives. You might be thinking to yourself at this point, "That's a No-brainer!", because the ideal choice that you feel they should be making might seem obvious.

But what if the relationship brought a sense of hope or a breath of fresh air in the midst of undesirable circumstances? What if in some little way it appeared to be the safe haven that was needed at the time?

Many people find themselves in these circumstances, especially when they feel like they have found someone who practically brings out the best in them. Through colorful and meaningful conversations, a person might be bombarded by the tapestry of what could be categorized as high-end compliments, canceling all the negatives that they might be facing in their lives at the time. Although these are the situations that some people on the outside looking in might envy, they might come with heavy price tags that most people don't see. They are usually camouflaged by the apparent bliss that shows up on the surface.

At times in these relationships, individuals have to endure the harsh reality of not being able to have their significant other to themselves. There is always someone else vying for the attention of the other party, therefore the relationships reach to a point where they cannot go any further. What's even more alarming is the fact that very often the person who they find themselves competing with, is legally bound to the person who often brings them the breath of fresh air that they feel that they need. Therefore they remain dedicated and loyal while enduring through the ups and downs that every relationship goes through. Then the choice to let go of them doesn't appear to be that simple.

~~~~~~~~~~

A quick glance at such relationships, and from the outside looking in, it would be very likely for anyone to see endurance in this case as a great quality, as it could be easily seen as a display of true dedication. These are valuable qualities to have in the area of relationships, and the actions that are sometimes taken could be highly admired. Many people looking in only wish they had the will to possess a mere fraction of these qualities themselves, in order to endure difficult times.

On the flip side, some people could become so used to having to go through the same thing every time, that they convince themselves that their choices and consequences are both inevitable, as they perceive that it might somehow be the normal or 'right' thing to do.

A deeper look into relationships of this nature could unveil that repeated actions and choices could very well be indicative of an underlying yearning that has found itself buried deep within their hearts. Could it be that the need to be in a close intimate relationship is felt in order for this yearning to be satisfied, even if it meant ignoring everything that goes against a person's own desires or standards? Or could there possibly be a need for the warm affections, affirmations and attention from another person, that is readily accepted even when it means doing it within a situation of compromise?

What kinds of experiences could such persons have endured early in life that would potentially cause a breakdown in their fulfilment as adults? Where are the missing pieces to their puzzles?

Very often we unconsciously hide our greatest need by choosing to remain in situations that we know deep down are not good for us, and rather than coming to terms with what we really need, we tend to mask it with our seemingly positive attributes such as dedication and loyalty.

Can dedication be used as an escape of what is really going on within a person? Could commitment be hiding a void that is buried deep within? Let us take a look at another example.

~~~~~~~~~~

Have you ever known someone who was so dedicated to their exercise regimen and healthy lifestyle that you can't help but wish you had the same motivation and level of commitment as they? Especially when you could actually see the nicely toned body and physical appearance that comes as a result? But what if having an ideal weight and toned muscles were not the motivation behind them remaining committed to their diets and exercise regimen?

Somewhere during this person's childhood, they might have developed an idea that only people with a particular body type get a certain level of attention from those of the opposite sex. Having this haunting thought throughout the adolescence years could very well produce a desire to be admired from an outward appearance. This idea and desire is taken well into adulthood, where the individual have tendencies to judge their beauty or how handsome they are, based on who notices them, or how able they are to 'turn heads'.

This type of mindset can in turn propel such persons to develop a lifestyle that would produce the kind of appearances that warrants the level of attention that is sought after. They find what works for them and they stick to it. Therefore what is seen on the surface is their high level of commitment, their dedication and what appears to be their discipline, hiding those inert fear of not looking good enough, and the low self-esteem that lingers in the corners of their minds.

~~~~~~~~~

Although this type of lifestyle could be admired and is highly commendable, as there is absolutely nothing wrong with wanting to look good and stay in shape. However, no one sees the thoughts that one could be battling with on the inside. On the surface it appears that they have it all together and that they are great examples to follow in keeping up with a healthy lifestyle, because they are faithful to their regimen. However, a deeper look would unveil a yearning that is possibly being carried from childhood into adulthood. A yearning that they feel can only be satisfied by what they do.

Just as The Woman at the Well had repeatedly gone to the well in an effort to do that which brought her what she perceived as something that was truly satisfying, in both examples, we see that people do what they feel they need to do in order to maintain that level of comfort and satisfaction. In these scenarios, (and there are many more that could be unveiled), the thirsts that these individuals experience are not very apparent on the surface because their actions are highly commendable, and could be seen as very normal. It takes a deeper look to figure out that their good intentions and actions are only there in an effort to quench a thirst and cover up a longing that is buried very deep within. No matter how good and how normal a person's actions might appear, they could very well be direct indications of a void that they have within, and the very things that they do in order to fill it. For this very reason, there are so many people who are seen as being very successful based on their level of education or financial status, but are some of the most un-happy people you could ever meet. What is seen is only what they use to mask what is really going on inside them.

On the flip side, there are also times when the behaviors that some people display are unacceptable, but they too are mere indicators of a thirst that they are experiencing deep within, and sadly, it is not always readily recognized. It would take some greater effort and a closer look to be able to see and determine that there is an underlying need that they have; one that they have set out to fulfill, as in these examples.

~~~~~~~~~~~

Growing up in a world where the concept of beauty is attached to an image that many people try their hardest to attain, regardless of the features that they were born with, could lead to the breakage of a person's self-image and worth. When a person is constantly teased and called names that are negative connotations toward their physical appearance, it can cause them to become very self-conscious and may carry around haunting feelings of inferiority as they measure themselves up against others of like age and gender. This is especially the case when they feel as though they are not ever noticed by anyone of the opposite sex.

According to the lenses that they are viewing their situation through, they eventually sum up their chances of ever nailing down a love-relationship with someone of the opposite sex as very slim to none. What can happen to such a person when there is a glimpse of hope when someone finally notices them, but only long enough to say hello and break their hearts when they realize that the love interests are not nearly mutual? Every glimpse of hope quickly fades, and despair continues. This is the sad outlook that some people have everyday of their lives.

Sometimes in cases like these, a person might receive the type of attention and affection that they always desired, from someone of the same gender. At first they might reject the thought, but soon become satisfied with how important that person makes them feel. Before you know it, they have begun to comfortably entertain same-sex relationships, which spirals into a way of life that they once despised.

Likewise, the ability to make such a choice could also stem from the way that a particular gender is perceived based on something traumatic that has happened in the life of a person. For instance, if that person witnessed or experienced for themselves very harsh treatment by some one of a certain gender, it is possible that that person might develop a strong hatred for the gender entirely, rather than for the one person who did the wrong. Again, this type of outlook could cause someone to gravitate toward a particular gender while shunning the other. It is therefore highly likely that they would turn to someone of the same sex for all relations.

The epidemic of gender-identity issues that has infiltrated many societies around the globe, has affected relationships, families, churches, schools and many other facets of life among a wide cross-section of individuals. We are constantly bombarded by the free expressions of persons who have made a choice to explore and lead a lifestyle of a transgendered nature. Although it is highly despised in some societies, some individuals find themselves on a steady path to this lifestyle.

~~~~~~~~~~~~~~~~~

In some societies that have strong Christian roots, we do not have to look very far to determine that this way of life is extremely undesirable and hardly tolerated, especially around the religious arena. Can you imagine the ridicule? Although this behaviour is despised on many levels, and is biblically and socially labelled as wrong, this can sometimes become a way of life for such individuals. What adjustments in one's past could prevent a person from travelling down the road of having gender-identity issues? Could normalcy come from other choices that could have been made? What sort of interventions could be used to transform a person's thoughts about him/herself?

Another example of how undesirable actions can point to a deep thirst within is described next.

~~~~~~~~~~~~

While many couples are experiencing true marital bliss, it is true that there are some marriages that are also on the brink of divorce. For some societies and religious circles, this is hardly an option when it comes to maintaining high moral standards of living. Regardless of what it might look like, even after a significant amount of years of marriage, one party might see divorce as the only option, while the other has made a conscious effort to fight to stay.

Having absolutely no interest in saving the marriage could be seen as being unreasonable and unfair. On top of that, what if that one party has found a love interest in someone else while the divorce process is in effect but not completed? Is it right to fall in love with someone else right at the end of decades of sharing a life in marriage with someone else? What if that person finds in that individual all the things that they were denied, or was lacking within the marriage? Is it natural to gravitate toward the relationship that provides a feeling of fulfillment? Or the one that provides compensation for what appeared to be lacking in the previous, even if it is superficial?

The new experiences of care, support, attention and affection is happily welcomed to replace the abrasive tones of commands and disrespect that a person might have experienced within the marriage. All that was desired for so long, is finally available and accessible in someone else. With time, strong feelings are harnessed around the new found love, while the marriage plummets to a daunting end. Surely that person has done the un-thinkable, and the risk of being ostracized is great.

~~~~~~~~~~~

Looking at a situation like this, it is very likely that one would see such actions as being unreasonable and disloyal, especially in a religious atmosphere. The thing that others are usually not able to see, could be the very thing that can push someone away from even wanting to continue in marriage. Whether or not there is a legal union between a man and a woman, is it possible that there really isn't any relationship? What factors can play into a person that is married gravitating toward someone other than their spouse? What could be the driving force behind 'outside' attractions? Although strong feelings could be harnessed during interactions with 'outside' individuals, having a thirst could present a valid question of what is actually felt when it comes to these types of attractions. Is it true love? Where are these feelings really coming from?

Do these situations sound or feel familiar in any way? Could it be that you are doing what you are doing because of an underlying thirst that you had been experiencing unknowingly? You might not fit into any of the examples outlined above, but you might be engaging in activities that have become the norm or way of life for you. If deeply assessed, they could be true indicators of something that you are thirsting for. These include, but are not limited to: Acquiring all the education or degrees that you can in order to feel some sense of importance, or pursuing titles and careers that might give some level of power and authority, in order to feel respected or give the inclination of being better than others.

Parents might also find it very necessary to cater to, or go out of their ways to make decisions that appease their children, in order to take care of feelings of fear or guilt of not being a good enough mother or father. Their actions might seem commendable, but if the truth is told, they could be unveiled as true indicators of a great thirst that needs to be satisfied in one area of their lives or another.

Why do you really do the things that you do? Take a moment to think about that. Sometimes the only way to identify a thirst that we repeatedly try to fill by actions that have become the norm is to allow God to search us and bring it to our attention. David's recognition of this is evident in this very heart-felt request he made to the Lord.

> *"Search me [thoroughly], O God, and know my heart! Try me, and know my thoughts!"*
> – Psalm 139:23(AMP)

> *"The idea is, search me thoroughly; examine not merely my outward conduct, but what I think about; what passes through my mind; what occupies my imagination and memory; what secures my affections and controls my will."*
> –Barnes' Notes on the Bible
> http://bible.cc/psalms/139-23.htm

There is no telling what we are really longing for until we sincerely and humbly ask our heavenly Father to search us and make us become aware of those deeply rooted motives that drive us to do the things that we do. Without that thorough search, we are left with our own limited ideas, opinions and sugar coatings of reasons why we do things that appear to be normal, and those things that just feel right. It is time to take the first step on the path to eternal satisfaction by taking a much deeper look. It will be worth finding out.

REFLECTION AND MEDITATION

"Search me, O God, and know my heart: try me, and know my thoughts."
-Psalm 139:23

After asking the Lord to search your heart, what are the actions that come to mind that might be indications of an inner void that you have been unconsciously trying to fill?

_____

_____

_____

_____

_____

_____

_____

_____

_____

Now that the motives of your actions have been revealed, what adjustments do you feel is necessary in order for your journey to finding life's fulfillment to begin?

_____

_____

_____

_____

_____

_____

_____

_____

_____

~ CHAPTER 2 ~

Private Practice

There are times when we really have to look deep within every crevice of our hearts to determine whether or not we are indeed thirsty. We have to really evaluate our actions and ask God to really search us to determine whether the things that we do repeatedly may serve as indicators of a void that we are forever trying to fill. Sometimes it takes thorough examination to be able to identify what we desperately yearn for, but truth be told, there are times that we know for certain what it is we are thirsty for, and are very much aware of the things that we do in order to seek satisfaction. The reality however, is that it might be more comfortable and convenient to keep that thirsty and parched area of our lives to ourselves, and that what we do in an effort to satisfy it, must by every means necessary, remain private.

Scripture tells us that the story took place at the well which the Woman at the Well had gone to draw water from, and seemingly at a time of day when no one would usually be there.

> *"And Jacob's well was there. So Jesus, tired as He was from*
> *His journey, sat down [to rest] by the well. It was then*
> *about the sixth hour (about noon)."*
> - St. John 4:6 (AMP)

According to Jewish time, the sixth hour was at noon, and if we know anything about noontime, we know that it is the time of day that the sun is directly overhead, which intensifies the contact of its rays. This could possibly mean that it was a very hot part of the day, if not the hottest. When the sun is blazing on a really hot day, most people prefer to be indoors. They would not choose to go anywhere at that time of day, and especially not with a heavy load.

It was the custom in the days that this story took place, that the Samaritan women went to draw water from the well in large groups at a time, and they did this at a time of day when it was much cooler. They would go in the cool of the evening, when they did not have to deal with the direct heat of the sun **(See Genesis 24:11)**. Not even by a stretch of our imagination was there the possibility of them driving to the well in cars with air-conditioning. They had to choose a time that was conducive to the necessary journey to get water for themselves, their families and any animals that they had.

I also imagine that these women looked forward to the time of fellowship as they walked together in the cool, to do their chore of drawing water. It must have been a special time, where they had the opportunity to talk and laugh with each other since they did not have the convenience of telephones, cell phones or social media that we have the luxury of using to communicate with others today. They might have used the time to share and to socialize while catching up on the latest happenings. This could certainly make the journey to the well much more enjoyable, and the burden of the daily chore a lot lighter.

Noontime was generally out of the question for drawing water, yet The Woman at the Well found herself along with her water-pot at the well, at the hottest point of the day. But why? Why would this woman possibly pass up the chance to enjoy the experience of fun and fellowship with the other women as they journeyed and drew their water together? Why would she go alone even if it meant having a greater struggle trying to manoeuvre through the lonely dusty streets under the scorching sun just to draw water from a well? It was a well that she had the rights to, and the luxury of going to at anytime. But why did she show up unaccompanied and at such an odd time to draw water?

In any attempt to answer this question, think for a moment about times when you would take a journey that you knew would end in gratification of some kind (even if it was just for a moment), but it was vital that you went alone. Or maybe it was in the comfort of your own home, but it was important not to let anyone in at the time when you would be performing that activity. Think about a time when you left your usual circle and ventured into territories that you could not possibly tell them about, just to get a fix of that thing or that person that you felt would give you just what you needed at that moment in time. For some people, it may not be a physical place, but possibly a place in their minds that they go to, in order to feel that sense of satisfaction that they long for; that place of reminiscence that stir those same feelings of gratification that were once felt in the past. This private place could also be manifested through the memory of those moments that many people so often re-live whenever they need that fix. It could also be the flood of thoughts that are welcomed and ravished in, that bring about those feelings that are so often desired to be in the present reality for many people, even if it is toxic to their lives and spiritual health.

Regardless of the action, we could all think of moments when we practiced them privately. We cannot dare lose the comfort in our so-called reputation by allowing anyone to know what is really going on inside our hearts. Those particular areas of our lives are parched and dry, and are in constant need of some satisfaction, and we are convinced that we are alone whenever we seek to find it. But are we really alone?

The psalmist David eloquently expresses it like this.

> *"Where can I go from Your Spirit? Or where can I flee from*
> *your presence? If I ascend into heaven, You are there; If I*
> *make my bed in hell, behold, You are there."*
> **–Psalm 139:7-8 (NKJV)**

The Woman at the Well planned to be alone, but instead, she met Jesus sitting on her temporary source of satisfaction, waiting for her arrival. Although she had it all figured out in her head, exactly where, when and what she had to do to get her thirst quenched, she had no idea that she would run right into the encounter that would indeed change her life forever, by giving her something that would take care of all her inner needs once and for all.

Think for a moment about your 'private practice'. Are you secretly welcoming toxins into your life? Are you secretly caught up in your own fantasies, that if anyone found out it could cost you your reputation? If you are like the Woman at the Well who purposely travelled to her *place* of temporary satisfaction alone, then you are in need of the only *encounter* that could put an end to your 'private practice'.

REFLECTION AND MEDITATION

*"For it is a shame even to speak of or mention the things that
[such people] practice in secret. But when anything is exposed
and reproved by the light, it is made visible and clear; and
where everything is visible and clear there is light."*
– Ephesians 5:12-13 (AMP)

What 'private practices' have you entertained in an effort to attain the
level of satisfaction that you seek?

_____

_____

_____

_____

_____

_____

_____

_____

_____

_____

How could these actions affect your reputation and God's purpose for
your life if they were brought to light?

_____

_____

_____

_____

_____

_____

_____

_____

_____

_____

CHAPTER 3

Extraordinary Encounters

One of the most amazing observations that I continue to make everywhere that I go, is the awesome creativity of God, to be able to come up with so many unique features and qualities that distinctly separate each member of the same species from the other. The human race is so vast, yet every individual that make up that great number, is very unique in many ways. I take note of this whenever I am in a place that is infested with people from all walks of life. I do this when I am walking in a mall, a grocery store, or better yet, the state fair which I happened to be at just a few days ago. I mean, there were people everywhere. They were on rides, standing around in groups or waiting for their order of the mouth watering foods that filled the air with an amalgamation of aromas. The delicious smells drew large crowds to the vending booths where they were prepared, sold and served. Some were sitting and puffing on cigarettes while others enjoyed the view of friends, relatives and others with the look of terror plastered on their faces. They watched as people were jerked and tossed about on some of the rides that could evidently be labelled as popular attractions at this fair.

No matter what they were doing, there were people all around, and each of them was different in very distinct ways. In addition to their very uniquely designed physical features, from their faces and skin color to their body structure and hair length and type, there was a mix of different ethnicities and cultural backgrounds represented there. If I were to begin to describe all of the intricate ways in which they were different, the list would be too great in length.

The truth of the matter is that we are all very different from each other, and it is because of those differences that we are able to tell ourselves and one another apart. In the midst of our differences however, there are significant similarities that aid in the forming of groups and other social and cultural circles. In other words, we tend to gravitate to the people who are similar to us in one way or another.

According to the article, *"Rules of Connectivity"*, the similarity theory states that familiar objects are more liked than less familiar ones, which also suggests that the same holds true when it comes to people. There is a natural tendency to favor persons who share a commonality whether it is in the area of opinions, personality traits, backgrounds, or lifestyles. Studies also support the idea that we tend to like and are attracted to people who are like us, and with whom we can relate.

http://westsidetoastmasters.com/resources/laws_persuasion/chap5.html

For example, I was once employed by a company who had a fair mixture of people who were either African American or Caucasian in ethnic background. It was either one or the other, except for one employee who happened to be Asian. Although there was this major difference, from what I could see, we all worked well with each other, and had developed bonds and great working relationships. I could recall however, one day we all went out to lunch at a nearby restaurant, where we had a wide choice of seats around a huge dining table that accommodated all of us. Without even thinking about it, people sat down around the table, but to my amazement at the time, I happened to notice that there was a direct separation between both ethnic groups, with the Caucasians seated on one half of the table while the African Americans were seated on the other. More interesting was the fact that the Asian employee found herself at the actual point of separation on one side, while another employee who was engaged in a bi-racial relationship, on the other, where the direct separation between the both groups occurred. Although there was no segregation necessarily in regards to the social climate around the lunch table, it was quite evident that the similarity theory was displayed that day, because unconsciously, people gravitated toward others who shared a commonality in ethnic background.

Far beyond our ethnicity however, each of us, based on our innate social preferences, have created circles with people whom we feel we could best relate to. They might be people who share certain things in common, such as lifestyles, careers and even in the area of economic statuses. Very often the bonds of these circles are so tight that we somehow push away or keep people who appear to be different from getting in. We keep those such persons at arms length to ensure that they do not interrupt the level of comfort that we have created for ourselves in the people whom we choose to associate with. As a result, we develop barriers that could potentially keep out not just people who are different, but also those very ones that were divinely sent to bring us exactly what we need.

> *"A Woman of Samaria came to draw water. Jesus said to her, "Give Me a drink." Then the woman of Samaria said to Him, "How is it that You, being a Jew, ask a drink from me, a Samaritan woman?" For Jews have no dealings with Samaritans. Jesus answered and said to her, "If you knew the gift of God, and who it is who says to you, 'Give Me a drink,' you would have asked Him, and He would have given you living water."*
> **–John 4: 7, 9-10 (NKJV)**

On one of her usual trips to the well, The Woman at the Well had been graced with a very unusual and in a lot of ways, extraordinary encounter. Now, I imagine that it was her intention to do what she would usually do at the well on one of her visits - perhaps rest a while, fill her water-pot and then head back home. Little did she know, her normal routine would soon be interrupted by a simple request of a stranger that she met there on this particular day. Jesus, who was sitting by the well when she got there, had asked her for a drink. From the woman's reply, we could tell that she was not very welcoming to having any company at the well. Not that of another person, and especially not that of a Jew. She was actually taken aback by the strange request. So instead of honoring it, she questioned Jesus' initiation to having some form of interaction with her.

On his way from Judea to Galilee, Jesus decided to pass through the city of Samaria. This was quite unusual for a Jew to even venture through there, although it was the shortest route to get from Judea to Galilee. Jews and Samaritans hated each other, and so they would usually take the longer route to avoid having any dealings with each other. With this in mind, and being who He was, Jesus still made it a point to pass there. It was not because it was required, but it was rather to satisfy His Divine intention.

> *"Now, He [Jesus] **had to** go through Samaria."*
> **–John 4:4 (NIV)**

It has already been suggested that He could have used the usual route to get where He was going, therefore it is important for us to understand that His encounter with this woman was premeditated. Hence the phrase, "had to". Knowing the kind of relationship that Jews had with Samaritans, it was not only unusual for a Jew to be seen there, but Jesus had the audacity to ask the Samaritan woman for a drink. Bear in mind that this request was not merely made to gain assistance or to simply make conversation, but rather, in His omniscience, Jesus knew of her *'need'* and He **purposed** to fill it.

God sometimes goes beyond and even breaks down social barriers in order to meet us at the point of our needs. The problem is, very often we do not recognize this, because of the method that He may choose to use. At times, we may encounter people that are not a part of our social circles, and may not meet the criteria in order for us to freely let them in, so we either ignore or turn them away. We inwardly question and oppose even the very thought of interacting with them on any level that would require letting them into our inner circles. However, just as it was in our story, these might be the very persons that God has sent our way, fully equipped to deposit what we really need, but we continue to miss out on this manifestation of God's provision and blessings in our lives because of the social walls we have built up around us.

You may be able to think of at least one person who you refused to let into your circle at some point, simply because of how different they were from you. You did not feel like they really fit in, but could that person be holding the key to the inner satisfaction you so desperately need? It might be in the form of a simple word, gesture, idea or random act of kindness. The truth is, you will never know, if you have those social barriers built between you and them. What blessings have you been missing out on by not accepting that person? Changing or expanding your circle could potentially add meaning and value to your life by accepting what God has sent your way through those that you need to embrace. Think about what the woman of Samaria would have missed out on, had she let the innate enmity between Jews and Samaritans cause her to leave her blessing behind and returned the way that she came to that well.

~ REFLECTION AND MEDITATION

"The Lord doesn't see things the way you see them. People judge by outward appearance, but the Lord looks at the heart."
- 1 Samuel 16:7b(NLT)

Who have you rejected from your social circle based on how different they appeared to be from those you would freely welcome?

_____

_____

_____

_____

_____

_____

_____

What changes can you make to your social boundaries that would make room for all who God might send your way?

_____

_____

_____

_____

_____

_____

_____

_____

~ CHAPTER 4 ~

Life and Light - Oasis or Mirage

It was not until after the barrier had been broken down, that the Woman at the Well was free to receive what was in store for her through her encounter with Jesus at the well - the encounter that brought change to her life in many ways. But what was it that Jesus came to bring to this desperate and thirsty woman of Samaria?

> *"In Him was life, and that life was the light of all mankind."*
> **- John 1:4 (NIV)**

The Woman at the Well hit a point in her life where she was experiencing desert conditions. She had come to a place of dryness, which made her existence very parched and arid. From her perspective, there was seemingly no evidence of a life worth living, or anything fruitful that could come out of it. Her life as she knew it was rid of anything that would give her the assurance that she needed in order to experience true fulfillment. Each time she thought that she had found a place of love and support that could propel her to truly experiencing the kind of satisfaction that she so desperately needed, she found herself having to pack up and leave when what she perceived as the next best thing came along. She did this repeatedly, not realizing that she was actually entering the same stage, using the same script and being influenced by the same cues, although she was employing a different cast. As another form of vernacular would put it, she was laying with the same devil that was only dressed in different clothing. But how could she not notice? How could she be so blind and naïve? Like many others who move from relationship to relationship only to be lured into the same mess, she had perhaps attached a clearance discount on the value of her own life, because everyone else failed to see what she was really worth.

Jesus, being omniscient, asked her to go call her husband. This woman has had a history of bad relationships, where she was constantly leaving one to go to the other, perhaps in search of something that only an encounter with Jesus could give to her. Could it be that she was in search of the stability and support that are sometimes necessary to sustain life? Was it the need for someone to affirm her life as valuable and worth living, by something she needed to hear or experience? It was obvious that the life that she was in search of could not be found in any of the failed marriages that she had shared with men, who she thought had what it took to bring fulfillment to her. Not even a life with the man that she had in her life at that moment, who Jesus confirmed was not even her husband, was able to satisfy her needs. Her life was dry and very much lacking in more ways than she had even realized. She was experiencing a great drought which could potentially lead to great patches of deadness in her existence. Does this sound familiar?

Although this story is an account of what happened in the life of the Woman at the Well way back in bible times, the situation is very much alive today, and is the sad reality that exists in our own lives, or the lives of many of the people that we see and encounter each day.

Jesus came to bring her Life.

"If you knew the gift of God and who it is that asks you for a drink, you would have asked Him and He would have given you Living Water."
– John 4:10 (NIV)

The water that Jesus was referring to was the only thing that could sustain her during the dryness that she had been experiencing for so long. It is very interesting that Jesus made reference to water as the solution to the woman's problems, given the place where she met Him.

Wasn't she already at a place where she could get water whenever she needed to? Whenever she got thirsty? Notice that He did not just offer her water, but Living Water. If her life was filled with deadness, then the water that the Messiah had referred to was the Life that needed to be imparted to her through Him, in order for her to move from a life where she was merely existing to actually LIVING.

I am reminded of a desert which can be defined as any area in which few forms of life can exist because of a lack of water, or any place that is lacking in something. It is also defined as a region so arid that it can hardly support any forms of life. A further look allowed us to find that the word arid could be defined as barren or unproductive because of lack of moisture, or lacking interest or imaginativeness. If this also defines what you are experiencing in your life right now, then you might be sharing something in common with the Woman at the Well, and that is a life in the desert; a place where water from a *'well'* could never begin to change.

The Oasis

There is hope because, amidst your dry land, there is an oasis. The Webster Dictionary defines an oasis as "A green or fertile section in the desert which contains water." Therefore, there can still be life, even in a desert situation, because of the presence of water. It is green because it is living, and it can produce fruit because it is fertile. An oasis can therefore be seen as a measure of hope that can exist even in an area of dryness in your life. No matter how dead things may seem in your life right now, there is a possibility and a hope that you can stay alive and flourish in your existence. There is a place where you can find life; a place that can sustain you through the wilderness and desert situation that you might be travelling through today. And if nothing seems to be happening for you right now, there is still hope through the oasis where you are able to be sustained and nourished, so that you are able to do the things that you thought could not be done. Therefore, although there are areas in your life that are dry, there is a Spring of Living water in the midst of your dryness, where there is life, and you can produce the fruit that God has called you to produce.

REFLECTION AND MEDITATION

"I will open rivers in desolate heights, And fountains in the midst of the valleys; I will make the wilderness a pool of water, And the dry land springs of water.
–Isaiah 41:18 (NKJV)

What area(s) of your life is/are experiencing desert conditions?

_____

_____

_____

_____

_____

_____

_____

_____

_____

_____

What oases have you failed to recognize because you have remained focused on the dry areas of your life?

_____

_____

_____

_____

_____

_____

_____

_____

_____

_____

Jesus came to bring light.

"When Jesus spoke again to the people, he said, "I am the light of the world. Whoever follows me will never walk in darkness, but will have the light of life."
- John 8:12 (NIV)

"Light is that by which we see objects distinctly. The sun enables us to discern the form, the distance, the magnitude, and the relations of objects, and prevents the perplexities and dangers which result from a state of darkness."
- Barnes' Notes on the Bible
Bible.cc/john/1-4.htm

Can you imagine life as we know it without any forms of light? Our days would be filled with constant collisions, accidents and bruises as we bump into everything that happens to be in our paths. Simply chaotic! As a matter of fact, there would probably be an empty world, because light is necessary for all things to be made. No wonder it was the first call of duty at the beginning of creation. Before God spoke, the earth was dark. It is interesting to note that before anything else was created, that Light was first called into existence.

"Now the earth was formless and empty, darkness was over the surface of the deep, and the Spirit of God was hovering over the waters. And God said, "Let there be light," and there was light."
Genesis 1:2-3 (NIV)

In order for the Woman at the Well to receive life through the Living Water that Jesus had brought to her, He had to illuminate and make her aware of her spiritual state, and what she was actually in need of. He knew that in order for her to fully accept what He had to offer her, she needed to 'see'. She needed to understand and discern that she did not just have a need of physical satisfaction, but that she needed a spiritual one as well. He redirected her attention from her physical thirst to her spiritual thirst – the THRIST that resonated from deep within her; the thirst that had imprisoned her.

You see, she had no idea that she was in a state of darkness. All she knew is that she was living a life that she had grown accustomed to that she felt comfortable living. Although there were definitely some dead and dry areas of her life that was in desperate need of life and moisture, she was totally ignorant of this fact, and of this need that she had. Jesus, who declared Himself as being the Light of the world according to John 8:12, was able to illuminate her life, enabling her to see what she had really needed, and that the answer could only be found in Him, by Him and through Him.

"Thy Word is a lamp unto my feet and a light unto my paths."
– Psalm 119:105 (KJV)

Whether the Word of God comes to us through the God-inspired words written in the Bible, a prophetic word spoken by a man or woman of God, a sermon preached from a pulpit, or that still small Voice that we hear deep within our spirits, it comes to shine in our lives to show us where we are, and then lights our way so that we could see or know where we need to go. In the same way, the Words that Jesus Himself spoke to The Woman at the Well, opened her eyes which allowed her to see her state, while providing her with lighted directions to her oasis, even in the midst of her wilderness.

At times God deems it necessary for us to go through the wilderness in order for us to experience Him in ways that we would not have ordinarily welcomed or even noticed. He takes us through, perhaps, in order to protect and prepare us for the place He plans on taking us. The wilderness experience could be one that presents many discomforts, but God in His loving-kindness offers us many oases of hope that we could hold on to during our pilgrimage. More importantly, He offers Himself as a Light to guide us and to show us where we ought to go.

As great and as necessary as this light is for us to see where we are, where we need to be and the way in which to get there, there are times when we are disillusioned by what we think or perceive to be there.

The Mirage

Sojourners going through a desert might in fact experience the false hope of mirages. What they think is a reality for them, is only an illusion of hope and satisfaction from what appears to be an oasis. They end up putting in all of their time, energy and resources as they focus on getting there, only to find that in a matter of time, what they had set there eyes on and hoped upon, would seem to have disappeared upon arrival, leaving them even more thirsty and exhausted. On top of all that, the experience leaves them with a great deal of disappointment. Why would they be so sure of what they had seen, yet when they got close enough, they realized that what they thought they saw was never really there? Does this sound familiar? This is the sad but true case with a mirage. It is only something illusory; without substance or reality, and is caused by a refraction of light. Scientifically speaking, when light is refracted, it means that there is a change of direction or a *bending* of its rays.

How many times have we found ourselves going after something or someone that somehow seems like the right thing, only to find out that it really wasn't the best thing for us? At first, it seemed so right, with everything lining up in every way, yet after we have had so much time, money or emotions invested, we come to the sad realization that it just was not meant to be. This could be true in the case of relationships, business ventures, ministry or any other choices that we have to make for that matter. I mean, how could we have missed when we became so off-course? Could it be that the Light of God's Word for us was *bent* to suit our own lusts and desires that what we thought was real was only an illusion? Many times when this happens, we have lost so much, trying to go after what we think things should be, rather than what they really are. This results in us having to reverse or make further detours in our journey, which could potentially delay our arrival at the place that God has already prepared and intended for us get to. It is in this place that we would receive the best that He has purposed for us to have.

No matter which direction light travels, it illuminates. Therefore we have to trust and depend on the uncompromised Light of God's Word to light our paths in order for us to see our ways out of darkness.

This would enable us in a way that we could be guided and directed to Life. It will also determine where we will end up, and guarantee true life and hope from an actual oasis, rather than the illusions that are always presented by mirages.

REFLECTION AND MEDITATION

*"The people walking in darkness have seen a great light;
on those living in the land of deep darkness a light has
dawned."*
- Isaiah 9:2 (NIV)

Reflect on your life. Can you identify any mirages that you sought after? Describe an experience that was the result of a mirage in your life.

_____

_____

_____

_____

_____

_____

_____

_____

_____

From a previous experience, describe the dangers of compromising the Word of God in an effort to justify any of your own lusts, desires or actions.

_____

_____

_____

_____

_____

_____

_____

_____

_____

_____

~ CHAPTER 5 ~

H-2-O
(<u>H</u>ydration - to - <u>O</u>verflow)

*"Jesus answered, "Everyone who drinks this water will be
thirsty again, but whoever drinks the water I give to them
will never thirst. Indeed, the water I give them will become in
them a spring of water welling up to eternal life."*
– John 4:13 – 14 (NIV)

I s it really possible to be always satisfied to the point that we would
no longer be in need of anything ever in life? Once we receive
this Spring of Living Water, does this mean that life will not ignite
any desires and yearnings in us? Does it mean that we will no longer
experience any kinds of weakness or need?

Have you ever gone to turn on a faucet in your home only to find
just a drip? Then you realize that water is turned off city-wide? This
was a constant reality that took place in the country where I grew up.
Very often and unexpectedly, water would be turned off at times when
it was very much needed.

Just imagine having running water at the beginning of your shower,
and then by the time you are ready to rinse the thick soapy lather off
of your skin, all you get are a few drips of water from the same shower
head. Or think about doing your laundry and in the middle of the
washing cycle, water shuts off. Either of those two experiences was very

much undesirable, and at times it could also be very frustrating to find that when you needed water the most, there was no source of it around. Even if we remained proactive and filled up empty containers during the times when there was an abundant flow of water, there was still the chance of it running low, or completely out.

On the contrary, I had many opportunities to visit another island where the abundant flow of water was always guaranteed. It was a special luxury to know that no matter the capacity to which there was a need of water, there was the certainty that it was going to be supplied. Even if it was just to get a quick drink while walking, from one of the many faucets that were frequently and strategically set-up along the streets. Whenever they were opened, there was always an abundant flow coming out of them; more than enough to quench a thirst.

In both countries, the need for water was the same, but the experiences and the surety of always having that abundant supply were indeed very different. Therefore the question that remains is this. What caused the water supply to be so different in both countries? Why was there such a surety on one island, but a fear of not having enough on the other? What was the major factor that separated the realities and experiences on these islands?

This factor was what Jesus had addressed during His conversation with the Woman at the Well. What He was comparing was not so much the thirst, but rather the source from which we get our satisfaction in life. It is identical to the comparison between getting water from a dripping faucet, and from one that has an abundant flow of water; the comparison that was evident between the water supply on either island. You see, on the island where I grew up, there was a city plant that was responsible for dredging water from the ocean, treating it with chemicals that would remove the salt and other elements that made it too heavy for everyday use, and then distributing it to homes and businesses through an underground piping system. Residents and businesses were then billed according to the amount of water that they used, although they had to deal with the constant unexpected shut-offs. Pretty soon it became so frequent that it was expected to happen, thus becoming the norm. As a result, homes were built above cisterns that were used as an alternate source of water, and one that was more suitable for drinking. The water supply in the cistern was determined by how much it rained, or how much people were willing to pay to have truck loads of water delivered to fill it up. Either way, it was very costly to have running water, and there were no guarantees that you would have it when you needed it.

Not so for the island where I went to visit some of my relatives. The source of water there was a natural spring that was located high on top of one of the mountains. For this reason, there was a constant supply of water that sprung up from out of the earth and then ran through pipes that were used to channel the water to residential homes, street faucets and businesses.

We discussed in the previous chapter that water represents life and all that it has to offer. Bearing this in mind, we could agree that there will always be a need for it throughout daily living, and it would be safe to say that there is often a need for an abundant supply, in order to get things done. In other words, an overflowing supply of water enhances our lives in many ways, and always provides the means to do so. Try washing your hands under a thin stream or dripping faucet, and compare it with washing them under an abundantly flowing stream with just the right pressure. If you also think of the amount of time needed to fill one glass under a dripping outlet, and the time required to fill it under a heavy flow of water, you will see that there is a significant difference in the amount of time that you consume, just trying to quench a thirst.

Likewise, the thought of a sponge could help us to see the difference with what can actually be done when there is an abundant supply of water as opposed to simply being wet. When a sponge is dry, it is almost near to impossible for it to be used in the way that it was created and designed to be. It is very hard and very stiff, and will not be able to reach into those places that it is required to go into, in order to fulfill its purpose. Even if water is present by a few drops, it is still not able to perform at its maximum potential. That sponge has to be totally submerged in an overflow of water, where it is able to be squeezed to the desired wetness with just the right pressure, without losing its shape and tenacity, in order to fulfill its duties.

You see, our lives are in a lot of ways like that sponge, and many times we settle for merely being hydrated by the simple presence of water even if there is only a little in supply. What we really need is an overflow to keep us sustained and operating at the potential in which God designed for us in the beginning. When we are squeezed by the pressures that come with this life, instead of being bent out of shape in our thinking, attitudes and actions, we could rather maintain our flexibility and tenacity while accepting the process of preparation for the destinies that we all need to fulfill. We were offered an everlasting flow of what we need, from the Spring of Living water, yet we spend our time skimping from sources that could only give us enough to wet our appetites. We turn to things, people and ideologies to give us temporary satisfaction, instead of going to the place that has the abundance that we need to keep us eternally fulfilled. We even give out more and consume more of our time, energy and other resources by having to constantly and frequently return to particular sources just to get that quick fix. Yet after just a moment, we find ourselves still empty and unsatisfied.

It is time that we ask ourselves whether we simply want to live being merely hydrated, or whether we want the overflow that is guaranteed to keep us eternally satisfied. Should we continue to run to the well to satisfy or needs, or should we embrace the spring of Living Water that is available to us through Christ? It is a choice that is necessary in order to determine the degree to which we will be satisfied. Are you giving up the luxury of being able to access the ever flowing Spring of living water, for a few drips or sips here and there? Which would you really prefer?

REFLECTION AND MEDITATION

*"And do not turn aside; for then you would go after empty
things which cannot profit or deliver, for they are nothing."*
– I Samuel 12:21(NKJV)

What sources in your life have you been skimping from in an effort to
feel fulfilled?

_____

_____

_____

_____

_____

_____

_____

_____

_____

What decisions do you have to make that will take you from the place
of merely being hydrated to the place of overflow that is both available
and accessible to you?

_____

_____

_____

_____

_____

_____

_____

_____

_____

~ CHAPTER 6 ~

Wells vs. Springs

The well represents the things that like the Woman at the Well, we turn to for the satisfaction that we need deep in our souls. We all possess a great need of the Living Water that can only be found by accessing the Spring that God wants to be within us. We must then choose between the 'well' and the Spring. Here is what the Lord has to say about it.

> *"For My people have committed two evils: They have forsaken Me, the fountain of Living Waters, and made for themselves cisterns (wells) – broken cisterns (wells) that can hold no water."*
>
> **- Jeremiah 2:13**

WELLS

Wells are Man-made

Anything that is man-made is artificial. There is nothing natural about it. They are usually imitations to what is natural, and will never come with the same guarantees. It is never the real deal, but merely a counterfeit to what is truly authentic. It is like purchasing a low-end brand of a product, only to realize that you were better off buying the brand that gives maximum satisfaction, which is, in most cases, the leading brand, even though you might sacrifice more. Buying clothes and accessories is also another example of the difference in quality that you get when you purchase authentic brands as opposed to the imitations. To see the true quality of the imitation that you get, only time and a few washes will tell.

Likewise, the wells that are constructed by mere human hands could never bare the stamp of true quality, and could never guarantee the best and true satisfaction. It is by far, very limited in its ability to supply the best quality and amount of water, for as long as you will need it.

Have you ever seen someone from a distance and for some strange reason you had a desire to meet them, and once you did, you wonder what was so grand in the first place? It did not take too long before realizing that the whole idea of meeting and being in their company was not at all what it was cracked up to be. On the flip side of that, there might have been someone that you were a little iffy about meeting, and once you met them, you soon realized that they are one of the most authentic and genuine persons you have ever come across in life. Which do you suppose was the imitation of the real deal? Which one represented the imitating characteristic of a well?

Wells are Temporal

Anything that is made by man, will only exist for a time. Just as they have a beginning, they are as sure as there is a God, to have an end. By no means do they last forever, although they might appear that way. In life we have the privilege of enjoying the very things that we depend on to give us that sense of security and satisfaction, but if we dare to live long enough, we eventually realise that these things and their abilities to bring us any kind of satisfaction or gratification, do come to an end.

If you search your heart, or simply take inventory of your life, you will realize that you do not have to look very far in order to identify a well. What is that thing that you once depended on to bring you fulfillment that is no longer there, or might still be there, but no longer have that effect on you? Remember how you felt during the times that it satisfied? Now, that reality only exists as a figment of your past. Was it a position in a prestigious corporation which was accompanied by a salary that allowed you to buy anything that you wanted without having to think about it? During that time, your life felt very secured, because things were going well for the company, and you made sure that you put in that extra time and made huge sacrifices that were certainly being noticed by the ones that were responsible for handing out promotions. Although you were hardly able to spend much quality time with your family, you were convinced that your ability to create the life of luxury that you thought they wanted was able to make up for it. It was not before long, in the middle of your so-called secured life, that the economical status of the company took a nose dive, and the only position that you ended up with, was on the list of persons that were being laid off in order to keep the company afloat. Just when everything seemed to be going perfect, the rug was pulled from under your feet, and just as a person would fall, so it seemed like your entire world came tumbling down. This is how temporal and uncertain wells could be.

What about the spouse that you married or the person that you hooked up with? Before marrying or even having an intimate relationship with this person, you imagined that they would somehow provide the kind of unshakable security and satisfaction that you were looking for. Without any kind of warning, everything got shaken up, through either tragedy or an untimely end to the marriage or relationship. As a result, you find yourself in a swirl of feelings of discouragement, devastation and in some ways, handicapped.

In whatever ways wells are being represented in your life, it is important that you be reminded that they are only temporary, and as much as it appears that way, they will never last forever. Just ask the drug addict, who is always in pursuit of that 'high'. Although the feeling is described as a place of euphoria in light of the respite from the repercussions of undesirable conditions and emotional turmoil that is experienced normally, it never lasts. Before you know it, the addict is right back in the state of mind of needing to feel that 'high' again. This is the very similar fate of the person that runs to the well for any kind of satisfaction.

Wells are Faulted

Another thing that we need to realize about wells is that they are faulted. They are in constant need of repair of some sort, and they tend to leak, which makes it very difficult to hold any water. How very disappointing it would be to travel to a well expecting to gain from it the very thing that you desire to quench the unbearable thirst within you, only to find no water. Especially if you were able to get some form of satisfaction out of it during your previous visits. It is bad enough that you have to keep making frequent visits to the well in an attempt to maintain satisfaction, but it is so much worse to go there to find that what you got from it before is no longer there because everything has leaked out through cracks.

I remember once going into a store, and what I beheld as a beautiful and unusual piece of artistry, was enough for me to pick up the aluminium watering can that was sitting on the shelf with the other household items. To my surprise however, this watering can was not found in the section with all the other planting and gardening supplies, but rather, it was placed in the section with what appeared to be decorative items. It was a beautiful watering can with patterns of flowers and bumble bees indented around its body. It was like no other watering can that I had ever seen. I was always a sucker for things that were uniquely designed, but surely this would be ideal for me to use to water the few potted plants that sat on the rail of my second-floor patio. I smiled as I imagined myself watering those plants in style. "Green-Thumb, here I come!" I thought.

I hurried home as I was not able to wait to try out my new stylish watering can. As soon as I got inside, I rushed to fill the can with water, so that I could have some fun watering the plants. To my bewilderment and dismay, by the time I walked over to the patio, most of the water in the can had left a very wet and messy trail along the wet path that it had created along the way. There was water pouring from every seam of that can, and by the time I was ready to pour water unto the plants, there was nothing left inside the can. I was very disappointed, but then it dawned on me that this particular watering can was not designed to be used to actually water plants, but rather to sit as a decorative piece in a home somewhere. I had certainly misinterpreted the original purpose for the watering can, and as a result I created a very big mess, and my thirsty plants were still without water.

Life's situations can sometimes be like that watering can. The faults and cracks in wells could be identified as those situations that result from the misinterpretation of purpose. We very seldom, if at all, seek out what God's original purpose is for having us encounter different experiences that we go through in our lives. Do we ever stop to find out or discern what God's intention was for allowing our paths to cross with certain individuals? Have you ever wondered or questioned why we have certain abilities and talents? Or why we travel and see different places? The list goes on, but the truth of the matter is that we get so caught up doing life that we end up missing the very purpose for each moment that we encounter. Myles Monroe in his book "Reclaiming God's Original Purpose for your Life" puts it like this.

> "The key to understanding humankind's presence and purpose on Earth is to understand God's original intent... Intent can be defined as original purpose....If we do not properly discern intent, misunderstanding will follow. This is one reason why there are so many confused people in the world: we have misunderstood God's original intent... Misunderstanding intent guarantees a waste of time, talent, energy, gifts, and resources. Unless we know what God intended, everything we do will be a waste of time."
>
> **– Dr. Myles Munroe**

Does this sound like you? Have you wasted lots of time and money pursuing things, relationships, ministries, business ventures and so on, simply because of a misinterpretation of purpose and understanding?

We cannot lead effecting lives if we are not living according to God's original purpose. Many relationships that started out very fruitful have gone sour, simply because of the misinterpretation of purpose. For those that seem to be thriving through the misunderstanding, if the truth be told, there is a lot of conformity that takes place. The same is true for every aspect of life. The book of Proverbs states that:

> *"There is a way that appears to be right, but in the end it leads to death."*
> **– Proverbs 16:25 (NIV)**

In other words, without the correct discernment of the original purposes in life, misunderstanding, confusion and un-fulfillment are all inevitable. Eventually, the ultimate purpose will surpass your desires, and you will find that once that happens, there will not be anything else left to sustain or satisfy you, and you would have created a big mess of your life and possibly someone else's in the process. This is what I like to call the 'watering-can syndrome'.

Whenever you find yourself depending on a well that is faulted, the natural tendency is to find ways to fix or repair it. We attempt to make repairs both knowingly and unknowingly by the things that we do and say. None-the-less, the fact that repairs have to be made, means that there is a chance that you are trying to get something out of a situation that was designed to bring about a different purpose. Our attempts to make repairs are identified when we constantly have to make excuses that would somehow justify why things are the way that they are, and the usual tendency to always remain in a position where you always feel as if there is a great need to defend, even when you don't have to.

Have you ever felt the need to change yourself in order to create a better fit? What about having to suppress your own beliefs and values in order to sustain and remain at peace with the life that you find yourself living in? Some people even end up having to change their very course and direction of life, constantly having to pack up and move from place to place (not necessarily physical), while dismissing their goals and ultimately aborting their dreams. No matter what is done however, there is no satisfaction or fulfillment. Trying to fit into a situation or life that was not designed, intended or purposed for you is like trying to use a square peg to plug a circular hole. Nothing fits! There are gaps! Vital things escape! Subsequently, making repairs are those things that we do in order to conform or fit into the life that we are trying so hard to maintain, when what we really need to do is let go and depend on God to lead us to the only source that can sustain and offer us the security and fulfillment that we so frequently desire.

SPRINGS

Springs are natural, and anything that is a part of nature is God-made. They are authentic and original. The way in which they function may never be completely understood by the limited minds of humans, but they exist without the assistance of anything that we can offer. Springs are also eternal. Therefore it is ever-flowing, and there is a never-ending supply of water that can be found there. Each time that you visit a Spring, it is guaranteed that you will be supplied with what you've gotten there before. You will never be disappointed if Springs are your source of satisfaction. They are perfect. There are no flaws found with utilizing Springs, and there is no room for leakage or anything running out.

It is no wonder that Jesus intended to point the Woman of Samaria to Himself as the Spring of Living Water and TRUE satisfaction. He was also directing her away from the well that she exhausted, in search of something that it was not able to provide for her. After she came to the awareness that there was indeed something better, and that she could truly be satisfied, she was faced with the task of choosing between the well and the Spring.

"The woman said to him, "Sir, give me this water so that
I won't get thirsty and have to keep coming here to draw
water."
– John 4:15

Likewise, we have the same decision to make today. Will we continue to exhaust ourselves seeking out temporary sources of satisfaction in our lives? Or will we finally turn to the Spring of Living Water that is within us in order to find true fulfillment and satisfaction?

Springs can become contaminated

I was once giving someone the description of the Spring, and she challenged my position by reminding me of the fact that Springs can sometimes be contaminated. Facing this major possibility when it came to springs, I immediately began asking the Holy Spirit to shed some light on this. As always, He imparted His infinite wisdom as this fresh revelation surfaced during my meditation on the subject.

As believers we do possess the Spring of Living Water on the inside of us. Yet, it appears that it is either no longer there or it has no effect. You see, even though the Spring is pure, providing a never-ending flow of water, it definitely can become contaminated. When a spring is working the way that it should, water flows from the inside out. There is a particular aura that a person carries, when the Spring of Living Water is in perfect operation on the inside of them. This aura is present in the characteristics that will be seen in their outward displays in their thinking and everyday living.

> *"But the fruit of the Spirit is love, joy, peace, longsuffering,*
> *kindness, goodness, faithfulness, gentleness, self-control.*
> *Against such there is no law."*
> **Galatians 5:22–23**

Unfortunately there are contaminants on the outside that can potentially affect the quality of the water that is coming out of a spring. In other words, there are outside factors in a person's life that can alter the original characteristics that the presence of the Spring of Living Water can produce in their lives. This will in fact hinder any of the ways in which the Spring could benefit them.

You may be wondering where these contaminants come from, or what they really are. There is an answer. Our eyes and ears are the gateways to our souls. This is where contaminants find their way into our very beings, bringing change to the landscape of our minds and hearts. They come from what we hear and what we see. Therefore, if you are not experiencing the ultimate result of having the Spring of Living Water within, it is time to take a look, and pay very close attention to the things and people that we listen to, and what we allow our eyes to behold. Sometimes we do take in contaminants unaware, which also hinders that refreshing experience of having the Spring within. That is why it is imperative that we constantly go through spiritual cleansing or what I call a spiritual detox to get rid of unwanted contaminants such as worry, stress, doubt, lust etc., with the washing of the Word of God.

Likewise, the Spring could appear to be dried up when the flow seems to have come to an end. But does the flow really stop? Or is it simply being choked? When there are various forms of trash and debris blocking the flow of the Spring, it could definitely appear as though it has dried up. If you are not experiencing the flow of refreshing water from the Spring of Life within, then it might be time to check for the possibility of trash that might have surfaced and choked the flow. Some very common forms of trash are un-forgiveness, malice, practicing sin, and stinking thinking. These are a mere few items on a long list. However, they are a great place to begin dealing with and getting rid of the trash in your life, that has choked the flow of the refreshing that you need to experience in your spirit.

Getting rid of trash and contamination from our lives would potentially put us in a position where we can undoubtedly experience the benefits of having the Spring of Living Water within us. Hence we stand a great chance to be able to trade in our dry and thirsty hearts for one that runs on life and eternal fulfillment.

REFLECTION AND MEDITATION

*"For My people have committed two evils: They have
forsaken Me, the fountain of Living Waters, and made for
themselves cisterns (wells) — broken cisterns (wells) that can
hold no water."*
- Jeremiah 2:13(NKJV)

What are those things that represent the wells in your life?

_____
_____
_____
_____
_____
_____
_____
_____
_____

What are some of the contaminants and choking agents that have caused
the Spring of Living Water to appear to be inexistent in your life?

_____
_____
_____
_____
_____
_____
_____
_____
_____
_____

~ CHAPTER 7 ~

Drink

*"But whoever **drinks** the water I give them will never thirst.*
Indeed, the water I give them will become in them a spring of
water welling up to eternal life."
- St. John 4:14 (NIV)

The clear and clean Spring is in no doubt the choice that we should make, but even after choosing the Spring of Living Water, there is effort needed on our part in order for us to truly receive the benefits. Just like the Woman at the Well that Jesus said these words to, there is something that we need to do.

John 4:14 begins with the phrase, "Whoever drinks..." This is indicative of the open invitation that has been sent out. It does not refer to a particular group. No matter what gender, age, ethnicity, financial status or walk of life that got you to this point, the opening of this scripture refers to you.

"Come, all you who are thirsty, come to the waters; and
you who have no money, come, buy and eat! Come buy
wine and milk without money and without cost. Why spend
money on what is not bread, and your labor on what does
not satisfy?"
–Isaiah 55:1-2 (NIV)

Not only is the invitation open to all who are willing to receive and partake of it, but we can see that it is one that benefits us in more ways than one, and most importantly, it has in it the divine ability to truly satisfy. All we have to do is accept it and take full advantage. The truth is, you might find yourself in a position where you have exhausted your resources and energy trying to fulfill your desires. Why continue when you have a shot at being eternally satisfied? The best part is, you will always qualify to receive the invitation, and you are not required to spend money or perform any labors to receive it. The only thing it says that you need to do is "Come...!" This could in no doubt be the best invitation that you have ever had presented to you. Why not accept it?

Whoever Drinks...

The word 'drinks' is a verb. It indicates an action. Once we have accepted God's gift of salvation by faith, the Spring of Living Water is already within us. Now that we are aware that it is there, and that it is an option that we so often overlook when we, like that woman are in search of deep satisfaction, we need to stop and DRINK! It is not automatic! It won't just happen!

There is an old English Proverb that says:

"You can lead a horse to water, but you can't make it drink."

The implications of this old proverb have been relative for many generations, and its familiarity has transcended through time. Like many of the old sayings that we have heard repeated time and time again, we may not be able to tell of its origin, but without much thought we are able to identify with its meaning. I'm sure that you or someone you know has uttered these words at some point in time. Maybe you could even think of a situation to which it can be applied. For the sake of the very small percentage of persons who have never heard of it or those who are probably having a nose-bleed trying to figure out what it means, let me explain.

Often times we are faced with opportunities or perhaps the solution to problems that we encounter through daily living. They could manifest through a clear directive from God, an open door or even a significant offer that is made. Of course the list goes on, but what brings the meaning to life is the fact that there are so many of us that could identify these opportunities as answers to prayers, but rather than taking action and really putting them to work in our lives for the better, we simply stare at them while remaining stuck in the same situation. You see, nothing will ever change until we perform the action that would allow us to access and benefit from them. It's like standing at point A, needing to get to point B in order for things to change. Although it is visible, simply desiring to get there, stating all the benefits of getting there, and even believing that you can get there, will never get you there unless you take action – put one foot in front of the other, make strides that will eventually close the gap between where you are and where you need to be. Even if you decided to drive there, you will never get there until you take the car out of the 'Park' or 'Neutral' state, actually put it into gear and put some pressure on the accelerator. In every case, the answers are before you. The benefits are there. But you are required to do something in order to receive them. There are actions that need to be taken.

It is like having a table set before you daily with the most wonderful foods that you could possibly think of, and you end up starving to death. "How is that even possible?" You may ask yourself. I'm glad you asked, so here is why. You felt the hunger pangs, you felt when your taste buds were activated in preparation of great enjoyment, you even began salivating by the mouth-watering aromas that were coming from the foods day after day, but yet, you die. You see, although you had everything set before you, and your body was in full gear to enjoy great meals, you simply failed to EAT. In order to be nourished by the foods that are at our disposals, we MUST partake of them.

Are you stuck?

Whenever you are at a point where you simply need to take some sort of action in order to get the results that you desire, rather than actually moving forward, you sometimes remain stuck. Why do you so often fail to take action? What is actually stopping you?

People tend to get so comfortable in their situations, that even though they see that the opportunity for change and blessings are raining all around them, they simply stay put. If you are one of those persons, then you must know that if your blessings are raining all around, you will never get wet if you refuse to step outside of your place of comfort.

The children of Israel were in this same predicament in the accounts that were recorded in Numbers 14. God had delivered them out of Egypt where they had been enslaved for many years. He led them from there, through the wilderness toward a better place; a place that was flowing with milk and honey. It was a place where they would not want for anything. It was a place of abundance and promise. On their journey from slavery toward the promise land, the Israelites were first-hand witnesses of miracle after miracle that God had performed in order to provide nourishment for them and keep them safe. They had seen the manifestations of God's Power on a continual basis, and the favor that He had extended to them. Yet, when they finally came to their place of promise, rather than trusting God and taking possession of it, many of them remained so stuck that they never experienced the life that they had journeyed so long to get to. In fact, many of them had actually expressed their desire to return to Egypt. They actually thought that they were better off in their place of bondage. (**See Numbers 14:2-3**) Some of you reading this might be thinking to yourselves, "Are they kidding me? Are they serious? Are they for real?" But what would you have done if you were there?

The land of Promise was there for them. All they had to do was to possess it. Instead, they chose to remain in the same place, even desiring to go back to Egypt as slaves.

If given the opportunity to go back in time? How many of us would opt to go back to Egypt rather than joining Joshua and Caleb which were the only two who actually took possession of the land?

God did all that He needed to do to get them there, but it was up to them to do what was necessary to experience the goodness of the land, which was to simply take possession of it.

Although it is impossible to go back in time, many of you are facing your promise, but you remain stuck because you have simply failed to act. You know that the situation that you are in right now will never bring you the kind of satisfaction that you are looking for. You know that it is time to leave that well behind and Drink from the Spring of Living Water that God has already prepared for you in Him.

Don't spend your entire lives simply settling for less, when God wants to give you His very best! It is time to Access it!

It's totally up to us!

All that we need is before us. God is all we need. He wants to be and give us all that we desire, but unlike us, He is not forceful. He never forces us to do anything, even if our lives depended on it. We have to want it badly enough to do something about it.

> "Behold, I stand at the door and knock. If anyone hears My voice and opens the door, I will come in to him and dine with him, and he with Me."
> **–Revelation 3:20 (NKJV)**

He is continually knocking, pleading, calling and inviting, but if we don't go through with the action of actually opening that door, He will not force His way in. He has given us the privilege of choosing, and He desires for us to always choose Life. Whether or not we do decide to make a choice, not choosing anything is in itself a choice. Therefore, don't be fooled!

Throughout scripture, we are encouraged to take action. The following are just a few.

"**Come** and let us reason together… (Isaiah 1:18)
"**Ask**, and it shall… (Matt 7:7)
"**Seek**, and you shall… (Matt 7:7)
"**Knock**, and the door shall be… (Matt 7:7)
"**Call** on Me and I will… (Jeremiah 33:3)
"**Put on** the whole Amour of God… (Ephesians 6:11)
"…, **think** on these things." (Philippians 4:8)

Each of these actions is attached to a result of some sort, which indicates how much we are required to actually choose and take action. We could believe God's Word all we want, and have faith in what He is able to do, but if we do not make a conscious decision to perform the action, then our faith and belief are for nothing. We will never experience the awesome results that are waiting to overtake us.

Just take a look at the way that James the apostle puts it.

"Was not Abraham our father justified by works when he offered Isaac his son to the altar? Do you see that faith was working together with his works, and by works faith was made perfect? You see then that a man is justified by works, and not by faith only. For as the body without the spirit is dead, so faith without works is dead also."
–James 2:21-22,24,26 (NKJV)

I admonish you to put your faith in God's Word, and trust in its power to bring about the kinds of results that would give you the satisfaction that you so richly desire, but more so, I challenge you to go a step further and TAKE ACTION!

REFLECTION AND MEDITATION

"For as the body without the spirit is dead, so faith without works is dead also.
-James 2:26(KJV)

In what ways have you failed to take action in order to walk into the blessings God has brought to your life?

_____

_____

_____

_____

_____

What fears do you have that are hindering you from taking action toward God's promises in your life?

_____

_____

_____

_____

_____

What are some practical steps that you can take that will move you into the direction of possessing all that God has already made available to you?

_____

_____

_____

_____

_____

~ CHAPTER 8 ~

Let It Go!

"Then, leaving her water jar, the woman went back to the
town and said to the people, "Come, see a man who told me
everything I ever did. Could this be the Messiah?"
- John 4:28-29(NIV)

At the end of her encounter with Jesus, the Woman at the Well became aware of what she needed to be fully satisfied, and most importantly, the source of the eternal satisfaction that she had so desperately wanted. Her attempts to satisfy her inner needs came to an end when she realized that she had been seeking that satisfaction in all the wrong places. If you take a close look at the story, you will see that she did something very interesting, and at the same time, very profound, once she had found what she had been seeking all along. The scripture says that the woman left her water pot behind, and she went back into the town to inform everyone that the Messiah they had been waiting on was already on the scene. Once Jesus caused her to see where her real thirst lied, she quickly removed herself from the place of temporary satisfaction to a place of eternal fulfillment.

Sometimes we are brought to the realization that it is time to leave the source of our temporary satisfaction and move to the place that has been prepared to bring about the kind of fulfillment that we truly need and yearn for. However, in those instances where we try to move forward, we find ourselves holding on to bits and pieces of those elements that keep us reminded of what we were once able to receive from those particular places of temporary fulfillment. This is what I call the water-pot syndrome. Have you ever tried to get out of a situation that you know isn't good for you, but while making steps into the much needed change, you find yourself thinking thoughts of What-ifs? As you attempt to leave a place of familiarity and move toward the unknown, you tend to want to hold on to those little elements that help you to maintain a place of comfort. You hold on to that 'thing', just in case you may need to return. It also reminds me of an account that was recorded in the eleventh chapter of the book of Numbers.

On the way to their place of promise, the Israelites came to a place where they began to remember the very smells of the onions and garlic, and the thoughts of what they once ate in Egypt, the place of bondage that God had broken them free from. Rather than accepting the 'manna' that God had prepared to sustain and satisfy them, they let their memories of what they had to eat in Egypt, cause them to want to return, even though it was their place of bondage. (See Num. 11:5-6)

The Woman at the Well knew that if she had left the well (her place of temporary satisfaction) and held on to the water pot while trying to embrace the new place of eternal fulfillment, she would always be reminded of and would maintain a desire to return to the place that she needed to move away from. It's like trying to drive forward, but rather than looking through the huge windshield at what's in front, in life we keep our eyes focused on the tiny rear-view mirror, which can only give us a view of what we are leaving behind. Any attempt to move forward would be a recipe for a crash waiting to happen, which could turn out to be very fatal. Therefore, she kept looking forward, and made a clear decision to part with the very element that would keep her attached to the well. She left her water-pot behind! It means that she had come to the realization that she no longer needed it to get what she once hoped would give her the satisfaction to the yearning that she had been experiencing for most of her life. What the water-pot represents in the process of moving from a place of temporary satisfaction, is the avenue that is used to gain access to those things that we lean toward to fill the void that is felt deep within. It could be an object, a thought or memory that you replay over and over in your mind, or even an idea. Sometimes it is a person or a relationship. It is the very idea of going back. Through her extraordinary encounter, the Woman at the Well was able to bring herself to the point where she no longer needed to rely on those things and people that could only bring her temporary fulfillment. I could imagine her saying to herself, "Been there, done that!" She made a conscious decision to remain moving forward, and left her water-pot behind.

Letting Go

One of the most difficult things that we would ever have to go through while trying to move forward, is the process of letting go. I recently went through an experience where I was forced to the point of 'letting go'. Although the event was very practical, the spiritual implications were overpowering.

I had recently purchased the latest generation of the particular phone that I was using. I'm sure that by the time you read this, there would have been several generations that followed, considering how quickly they come out. Needless to say, God used the phone I had to teach me a very profound and well-needed lesson. Like I said, I had the latest version of the software, and soon after, a new one was introduced, and every user was advised to go through the software update. For me, I was satisfied with the one I was using, so I was in absolutely no hurry to do this update. I was happy with what I was able to do with the phone despite the use of the older software. Other people who had experienced the change, shared their experiences and all of the wonderful things that their phones could then do. It made no difference to me. I was fine with what I had, until one day, the phone began malfunctioning. Soon I grew unsatisfied and decided to take the plunge and do the update. Little did I know, in order to perform this in a safe manner, a strong internet connection was required. At the place where I was when I made the decision to go through the update process, the internet connection was very weak and inconsistent.

Without thinking about it, I gave the phone the command to begin the process. At first everything was going smoothly, so I looked away for a few minutes. By the time I looked at the phone again, I realized that the process was interrupted, and the phone had gone into a recovery mode. While in this mode, the phone was not able to do anything at all. It was unresponsive to any thing I did or any buttons I pressed. I had to take it to the manufacturer and had them plug it directly into their system in order for it to be restored. Once it was restored, I soon realized that I had lost everything that was saved on the phone. "Ouch!" I know some of you are probably saying while cringing at the thought of something like this ever happening to you. Yes, it hurt! I was able to outline the circumstances, but the emotional terror and discomforts that I had to go through were unimaginable, and very impossible to capture at this time. None-the-less, it was a situation that God used to show me where a lot of us as His children are when it comes to the place that He has in store for us to walk into - The place of everlasting satisfaction. Of course, I asked Him to explain what it all meant, and while driving alone one day, He began to speak and explained it in this way.

"Phoenicia, I have so much in store for my children, but just like the phone could not function at it's greatest potential because of the outdated software, many of them are not able to reap the benefits of this new place because they are trying to function and operate from an old mindset. Rather than continuously beating that dead horse or constantly beating up on themselves when they are not able to attain those desires that I placed within them, they simply need to upgrade their thinking and renew their minds.

> *"Don't copy the behavior and customs of this world, but let*
> *God transform you into a new person by changing the way*
> *you think. Then you will learn to know God's will for you,*
> *which is good and pleasing and perfect."*
> **– Romans 12:2 (NLT)**

He went on to say,

"Some of them do realize the need for change, so they set out in their own strength, devoting all of their energy to trying to figure everything out, only to end up having to face many disappointments, delays and detours along the way. I need them to realize that the change that they are seeking can only take place through Me, but just like your phone needed a strong and consistent internet connection in order for the software to be updated thoroughly and accurately, there needs to be a strong, consistent and uninterrupted connection between our communications with each other, through prayer (which also involves listening) and constant meditation on My Word."

This reminds me of the Woman at the Well and how she was able to activate and walk into the 'new life' she had found. It became accessible once she had that face to face encounter with the Messiah, the only one who was able to make all things new for her. I thought about how going back into the midst of some of the same people who had ridiculed and ostracized her, suddenly became very minute when she found her new hope in Christ. Could it be that she was restored because she had direct contact with the Lord? That she heard from Him for herself? If you are reading this, God wants you to know that He sees your efforts that seem to be counted as nothing, and that your restoration awaits you. All you need to do is plug into Him and remain consistently connected. This will cause every hindering thought that has kept you bound and unfulfilled, to be brought low, so that you could overcome and access what has already been prepared for you.

As I continued to sit in my car that day, the Lord continued to speak to me about what I had experienced with my phone. He said, "Just like you had to go back to the manufacturer to get the phone out of the recovery mode, and how it needed a direct connection to the system in order to restart it, My children must connect with Me directly to get a jumpstart into the right direction. It might mean losing everything that they deemed important, as you did when all information was lost from your phone. I am aware that the letting go process is a difficult one, but rest assured that it is very necessary in order for My children to be able to access and receive from the new place of benefits that I have already prepared for them. The truth is, many of My children may never see the places and things that I have in store for them, because they refuse to let go of the former things that they tend to hold on to for comfort. Therefore, rather than moving forward and upward, the weight of those things will keep them back. They must say and behave like my servant Paul who said,

> *"Brothers and sisters, I do not consider myself yet to have taken hold of it. But one thing I do: Forgetting what is behind and straining toward what is ahead, I press toward the goal to win the prize of the upward call of God in Christ Jesus.""*
> **- Philippians 3:13,14 (NIV,ASV)**

After receiving this response, as I meditated on all that the Holy Spirit had shared with me that day, I grew more and more appreciative of going through what I did with all that had happened with my phone. It is truly amazing how God could use a simple everyday occurrence to teach something so profound, and as I thought of the Woman at the Well, I could see why she had to make that conscious decision to let go of her water-pot after her encounter with Jesus that day at the well. She did exactly what she had to do to activate and access the new life that was in store for her. She rose from the well, let go of her water-pot, and totally separated herself from it. She was able to begin her new life when she consciously left it behind.

What have you been holding on to? What is holding you back from entering into that place of eternal fulfillment? As your thoughts are being flooded with the very answer to these questions, ask God to give you the wisdom and the strength that you need to completely let go!

REFLECTION AND MEDITATION

"Remember not the former things, nor consider the things
of old."
– Isaiah 43:18(ESV)

What fragments of the past are you holding on to that are keeping you comfortable with the possibility of going back one day?

_____

_____

_____

_____

_____

_____

_____

_____

_____

How have those things kept you stagnant, or robbed you of your ability to move forward?

_____

_____

_____

_____

_____

_____

_____

_____

_____

_____

~ EPILOGUE ~

A New Thirst

Go with the Flow

A few weeks ago, I was transporting some teenagers to a shopping day at the mall. I knew that a couple of them were athletes, who were very successful in their events in the Track & Field arena, and so I had the very exciting thought of them one day competing in the Olympics. I saw it as a gateway to have one of my usual inspirational talks, so I posed the question to one of the girls that I had randomly chosen. I asked, "What are your goals for Track?" To my surprise and bewilderment, her response was, "I don't have any goals." In an effort to inspire, I asked, "What about the Olympics? Do you see yourself ever competing there? She immediately responded, "Whether I go to the Olympics or not, I'm good. I'm having fun doing Track. I'm just going with the flow!" I wanted to begin the lecture about setting goals and working toward them, but somehow the Spirit was not giving me the release to open my mouth. All that started happening was that the phrase "Go with the Flow" continued to bounce around my thoughts and spirit." It wasn't until a couple of weeks later that what God wanted me to get from it, was revealed.

The process of letting go also involves the giving up of our own ways, plans and agendas, and giving the Lord complete hold of the reins that will guide our lives in the ways that He would have us go. We can rest assured and stand on the Word of God which tells us that God has good plans for each and everyone of us. Sadly, we often live contrary to those plans when we refuse to give up the reins which require that we give control over to the Creator Himself.

If you are in that place where you feel as though no matter what plans you make, they always or more often than not seem to end up with one road-block after the next, you are not alone. It might mean that you need to take a step back and see whose plans are really in play - Yours or God's? I remember the many days when I would always confront the Lord and have these never-ending arguments with Him. Arguments about where I wanted my life to be vs. where He was directing it. It wasn't before I finally gave in and said, "Take the win Lord!!" that I began to experience true joy and peace within. What I was actually saying to the Lord was, "My life is yours, and therefore I give you full control." It was at that moment of complete surrender that I realized two things.

1) God ALWAYS wins!
2) His ways are BEST for me.

There are no guarantees that His ways are by any means the most popular or comfortable, but I can tell you that you will always see purpose around you, and His peace and joy are by-products of living according to His plan and purpose. It is the very reason why, amidst all that he was going through, Paul could boldly and confidently say:

> *"I've learned by now to be quite content whatever my*
> *circumstances. I'm just as happy with little as with much,*
> *with much as with little. I've found the recipe for being*
> *happy whether full or hungry, hands full or hands empty.*
> *Whatever I have, wherever I am, I can make it through*
> *anything in the One who makes me who I am."*
> **– Philippians 4: 11(b) – 13 (The Message)**

It is great to have plans in place and work toward fulfilling them. But it is even greater when we could be open to God's leading and direction, where He could order our steps according to His will. God doesn't expect us to live aimlessly and merely watching life go by. He has equipped us with instincts that give us enough clues to make plans that would potentially satisfy the purpose for which He has attached to who we are, and who He fashioned us to be. Therefore, it is imperative that we do not allow ourselves to live contrary to His leading and direction, even in making plans. In other words, "Go with the Flow"!

"A man's mind plans his way, but the Lord directs his steps
and makes them sure."
– Proverbs 16:9 (AMP)

Moving contrary to the tide will always bring about frustration, much disappointments and not to mention, lots of wasted energy. When the tide is flowing in a particular direction, it is much more beneficial to go with the flow rather than trying to fight against it. This theory is also very applicable to life and God's Will for our lives.

Are you exhausted from the fight of life? Tired of constantly running into road blocks and being bombarded by disappointments and misfortunes? Then now might be the perfect time to give up those reins to the Lord and go with the flow.

Don't get me wrong, walking in the direction of God's divine plan is not quite a bed of roses, nor does it always feel like a walk in the park, but no matter what you encounter along the way, there is always provision, protection and most importantly, God's Presence. Just ask the children of Israel who God led through the wilderness to get to their land of promise. (See Exodus 13:17-18) It might have been the most challenging, but from God's perspective and omniscience, it was by far the better route, and certainly more rewarding. They were protected from their enemies, fed when they got hungry and thirsty, and constantly accompanied by His Presence.

Our finite being will never be able to see or understand anything pass their limits, but we serve a God who is all-seeing and all-knowing. Won't it be so much better to give up control, trust and let Him lead?

> *"Trust in the Lord with all your heart, And lean not on*
> *your own understanding; In all your ways acknowledge Him,*
> *And He shall direct your paths."*
> **-Proverbs 3:5-6**

A New Thirst

Having the Spring of Living Water in our lives, free of contaminants and unwanted debris, could indeed set us on the path to receiving everlasting fulfillment and satisfaction. One important question that needs to be addressed at this point is that of the total elimination of thirst from our lives. Does being eternally fulfilled eliminate all thirst? Won't that dismiss our need for God as well? Does He really want us to get rid of all thirst?

> *"Blessed are those who hunger and thirst for righteousness,*
> *for they shall be filled"*
> **-Matthew 5:6 (NKJV)**

No matter how satisfied and fulfilled we become, we should always be in a place where we need God. Therefore it must be understood that eternal satisfaction is not so much achieved within a particular time and place in our existence, but rather, it is a way of life. As we go through life, our need for God is sure, and as we desire Him, we will continue to be filled. Hunger and thirst are both inevitable on our journey through life. Therefore, we must then realize that rather than trying to eliminate them altogether, we must come to the point of shifting our desires from the things, people, ideas and experiences that are all limited in their ability to supply and satisfy our needs totally. We need to redirect our thirst for what can and will always bring us eternal fulfillment and that is a relationship with God and living out His Will for our lives everyday.

> *"Come, see a Man who told me all things that I ever did.*
> *Could this be the Christ? Then they went out of the city*
> *and came to Him"*
> **- John 4:29-30**

The Woman at the Well who Jesus met in the city of Samaria came face to face with all that she needed. She found the answer to the many questions concerning her life that plagued her mind, and the deep emptiness that she felt for so long. She took hold of everything that He purposed to give to her, and immediately became new in her existence. Her encounter with the Messiah Himself infused life and purpose within her, and caused her desire to be shifted from all the wrong people and experiences that she welcomed in search of true satisfaction. Her new desire was to glorify God and live out His will for her life. As she did this with her words and actions, the scriptures tell us that the people left where they were and came to Him. You see, When the life that we live points others to Christ, and what we say and do affects positive change in their lives, then we have begun fulfilling God's will for us. Consequently, as Jesus explained to His disciples, this is what will give us true satisfaction.

> *"In the meantime, His disciples urged Him, saying, "Rabbi, eat." But He said to them, "I have food to eat of which you do not know." Therefore the disciples said to one another, "Has anyone brought Him anything to eat?" Jesus said to them, "My food is to do the will of Him who sent Me, and to finish His work."*
> **–John 4:31-34 (NKJV)**

We have journeyed with the Woman at the Well, and could certainly say that we have identified with her in one way or another along the way. My prayer is that as you've read and taken this journey, you have found your path to spiritual enrichment and life fulfillment. As this woman represents so many of us today, let us follow her lead by drinking from the Spring of Living water within, and moving forward on the path that has been set before us. Once we have done this, like the woman, we would be fulfilling our life's purpose, and enjoying the much desired state of eternal satisfaction.

NOTES

Printed in the United States
By Bookmasters